THE PERSONAL SUCCESS POCKETBOOK

By Paul Hayden

Drawings by Phil Hailstone

"Paul has succeeded in creating an overview of all of the significant aspects of personal development, and presented it in a digestible manner. The strength of the material is its appeal to the eye and the concentration span!''

Richard D. Moat, Founder, The Positive Change Foundation

DEDICATION
For Kara and Leah, my two greatest successes.

Teaching kids to count is fine, but teaching them what counts is best - **Bob Talbert**

ACKNOWLEDGEMENTS
Thank you to the originators of all the quotes and to all those who have motivated me over the years.

My apologies to the inspirational people whose names have become separated from their words through the mists of time.

Published by:
Management Pocketbooks Ltd
Laurel House, Station Approach, Alresford, Hants SO24 9JH, U.K.
Tel: +44 (0)1962 735573 Fax: +44 (0)1962 733637
E-mail: sales@pocketbook.co.uk
Website: www.pocketbook.co.uk

British Library Cataloguing-in-Publication Data – A catalogue record for this book is available from the British Library.

Design, typesetting and graphics by **efex ltd.** Printed in U.K.

The man who makes no mistakes does not usually make anything
Edward John Phelps

FOREWORD

By Peter Thomson
UK's leading corporate and personal development strategist

Paul Hayden has done it again!

In this brilliant book of self-discovery Paul explains the basic truths behind personal success. His thought-provoking and challenging ideas on every page prompt you to re-examine your beliefs, your values and your actions. Packed from cover to cover with common sense and usable ideas, this latest offering from Paul Hayden is a must for anyone who is interested in increasing their success.

From planning to persistence. From motivation to goal setting. From managing change to a proven success toolkit. Paul puts his ideas in such a clear, concise way that anyone can use them to achieve their goals.

As you read through this apparently simple, though deeply thought out, book you will easily be persuaded to re-examine your life, re-visit your goals and determine to take those actions which will see you achieve your heart's desires. Only read this now if you really wish to experience the joy of personal success.

> *Every person is a self-made person, but only the*
> *successful ones admit it*

CONTENTS

Any fact facing us is not as important as our attitude toward it, for that determines our success or failure

Norman Vincent Peale

INTRODUCTION

*Always bear in mind that your
own resolution to succeed is more important than any other one thing*

Abraham Lincoln

KNOWING WHAT YOU WANT

Have you ever wondered what separates successful people from others?

Successful people have taken time to think about and define what they want in their lives.

Many people find they are too busy to think about what they are doing and why. They do not have the time to stop and think about what really matters to them. Others hide under a cloud of doubt and disappointment which leads to a lack of ambition.

Everybody has the talent to achieve their own definition of success; few have the discipline to achieve it.

Success does not mean having lots of money, although that is often how we measure it.

Consider the following, for example ...

> *The difference between a successful person and others is not a lack of strength, not a lack of knowledge, but rather a lack of will*
> **Vincent T. Lombardi**

To laugh often and much;

to win the respect of intelligent people and the affection of children;

to earn the appreciation of honest critics and endure the betrayal of false friends;

to appreciate beauty, to find the best in others;

to leave the world a bit better, whether by a healthy child, a garden patch or a redeemed social condition;

to know even one life has breathed easier because you have lived.

This is to have succeeded.

Ralph Waldo Emerson

Success is not the result of
spontaneous combustion. You must first set yourself on fire
Fred Shero

HOW TO USE THIS BOOK

This book has been designed for you to use as a workbook and reference book to help you define and achieve success.

When you read it, **use** it. Make notes, complete the exercises, apply the techniques, take action and start achieving.

Refer to it daily for inspiration and reminders of the techniques, to keep yourself focused on your goals and your affirmations, etc. This will help you achieve and maintain your definition of success.

This book may not make you rich. However, if you use it properly it will enrich your life.

I wish you every success!

There are no shortcuts to any place worth going
Beverley Sills

SUCCESS CYCLE

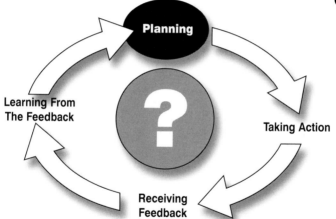

Planning

Taking Action

Receiving Feedback

Learning From The Feedback

?

The more time we spend on planning a project the less time is required for it. Don't let today's busy work crowd planning time out of your schedule

Ed Bliss

INTRODUCTION

Before you can achieve 'success' you must know what it is.

The Concise Oxford Dictionary
defines success as:

SUCCESS:
Accomplishment
of end
aimed at

Your definition of success
must be personal; it can
and will be different from
other people's.

You must, therefore, have an end in mind. Before you can achieve that end you must
know where you are starting from.

It's the start that stops most people

PLANNING

WHERE AM I NOW?

Take time to answer the following questions and work through the exercises to help you define where you are now:

What do I enjoy doing?

Why do I enjoy these things?

What don't I enjoy doing?

Why don't I enjoy these things?

What are my strengths?

What are my weaknesses?

What makes me happy?

What makes me sad?

The only limit to our realisation of tomorrow will be our doubts of today
Franklin Delano Roosevelt

WHERE AM I NOW?

MOTIVATORS

1. **Status**   - Seeking recognition/admiration/respect
2. **Power**   - Seeking control of people/resources
3. **Material rewards**   - Seeking possessions/wealth/high standard of living
4. **Autonomy**   - Seeking independence/ability to make own decisions
5. **Expertise**   - Seeking accomplishment in a specialised field
6. **Creativity**   - Seeking innovation and being identified with original output
7. **Affiliation**   - Seeking fulfilling relationships
8. **Search for meaning**   - Seeking things of value for their own sake
9. **Security**   - Seeking a solid/predictable future

*Those who cannot remember the past are condemned
to repeat it*

WHERE AM I NOW?

MOTIVATORS

From the list, select the item that
motivates you most (make a note of
the item at the back of the book).

From the chart, compare items
and place a ring around the number
that motivates you more.

1 or 4	1 or 3	1 or 2
1 or 5	2 or 5	1 or 9
2 or 3	2 or 6	2 or 8
2 or 7	4 or 7	2 or 9
3 or 4	5 or 8	3 or 8
3 or 7	5 or 9	4 or 2
4 or 8	6 or 3	4 or 5
5 or 6	7 or 1	4 or 6
6 or 7	7 or 8	5 or 3
6 or 9	8 or 6	5 or 7
8 or 1	9 or 8	6 or 1
9 or 7	9 or 4	9 or 3

Life is ours to be spent, not to be saved
D. H. Lawrence

WHERE AM I NOW?

MOTIVATORS

Add up how many times you have ringed each number. Put the totals in the grid.

No.	X
1	?
2	?
3	?
4	?
5	?
6	?
7	?
8	?
9	?
	=36

Indicate your order of preference below and compare this to the motivator you ranked highest at the beginning of the exercise.

No.	Motivator	Rank order
1	Status	
2	Power	
3	Material rewards	
4	Autonomy	
5	Expertise	
6	Creativity	
7	Affiliation	
8	Search for meaning	
9	Security	

How does this compare to the item you selected earlier as your top motivator?

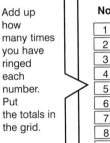

A turtle may live for hundreds of years because it is well protected by its shell, but it only moves forward when it sticks its head out

Ricardo Semler

WHERE AM I NOW?
ROLE MODEL

To ensure you cover all areas of your life, use the 'role model' on page 89. Take a copy of the model (as you will use it again later).

Put your name at the centre.

In the outer circles enter the various roles you find yourself in, eg: father, mother, husband, wife, daughter, son, brother, sister, friend, manager, team member, employee, employer, teacher, student, citizen, patron, volunteer, adviser, coach, consultant, etc.

Then, you can record where you are and how you feel about each of the roles you find yourself in.

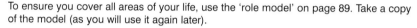

Life is a grindstone.
Whether it grinds us down or polishes us up depends on us
L. Thomas Holdcroft

DEFINING SUCCESS

With a clearer idea of where you are now, you can start defining where you want to be.

Take time to answer the following questions and work through the exercises to help you define success.

Ask yourself the following:

What do I want this year?

What do I want in five years?

What do I want in my lifetime?

Some day, when I get time, I'm going to ...

Invent the future instead of trying to redesign the past

DEFINING SUCCESS

MOTIVATORS

What do your top three motivators (on page 10) say about what success might look and feel like for you?

1. **Status** - Seeking recognition/admiration/respect
2. **Power** - Seeking control of people/resources
3. **Material rewards** - Seeking possessions/wealth/high standard of living
4. **Autonomy** - Seeking independence/ability to make own decisions
5. **Expertise** - Seeking accomplishment in a specialised field
6. **Creativity** - Seeking innovation and being identified with original output
7. **Affiliation** - Seeking fulfilling relationships
8. **Search for meaning** - Seeking things of value for their own sake
9. **Security** - Seeking a solid/predictable future

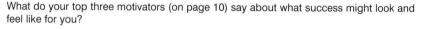

Anything the mind of man can conceive and believe, it can achieve
Napoleon Hill

(13)

DEFINING SUCCESS

Use another copy of the 'role model' (on page 89).

Do not refer to the previous model. Focus on what you want for the future.

Put your name at the centre, then complete the roles you want to maintain and those you want to adopt for the future.

For each of these roles record where you want to be and how you **will** feel about that role.

Ask yourself:

Why is this my ideal?

Is it realistic?

How does it compare to where I am now?

> *The future is not inevitable.*
> *We can influence it if we know what we want it to be*
>
> **Charles Handy**

DEFINING SUCCESS

Using all the work you have done you are ready to formalise your own definition of success.

Success is

A positive thought is the seed of a positive result

ASSESSING THE RISK

You get nothing for nothing in this world. It is important to recognise there will be a price to pay.

Are you prepared to pay the price of success?

ACTION NEEDED

The price:

Pain	Conflict	Struggle
Hard work	Loss	Time
Discomfort	Setbacks	Money, etc

If it was easy everyone would do it. The easy bit is staying in your comfort zone.

NO EFFORT

If you are not prepared to pay the price:
1. Reconsider your definition of success.
2. Put this book away until you are prepared to do so.

Slumps are like a soft bed. They're easy to get into and hard to get out of
Johnny Bench

ASSESSING THE RISK

Ask yourself:

- *What do I stand to gain?*

- *What could happen if I fail?*

- *Could I cope with the worst consequences?*

- *What will I learn?*

- *What would happen if I took no action?*

- *Are there any possible alternatives?*

- *How can I increase my chances of success?*

None but a fool worries about things he cannot influence
Samuel Johnson

ASSESSING THE RISK

To laugh is to risk appearing the fool
To reach out to another is to risk involvement
To place your ideas, your dreams before the crowd is to risk their loss
To live is to risk dying
To try is to risk failure
But the risk must be taken, because the greater hazard in life is to risk nothing
The person who risks nothing, does nothing and is nothing
He may avoid suffering, but he simply cannot learn, feel, change, grow, live
Chained by his certitudes, he is a slave
Only a person who risks is free

Take a risk

The trouble is, if you don't risk anything, you risk even more
Erica Jong

COMMITMENT

To achieve your definition of success
you're going to have to be committed.
How committed are you?

The hen had input
The pig was committed

We will either find a way, or make one
Hannibal

COMMITMENT

If you are prepared to pay the price, it means you think it's worth the risk and you are committed. You may still think there is something else holding you back, so remember:

- Beethoven wrote the world's greatest music when he was deaf.

- Milton wrote the greatest literature when he was blind.

- Winston Churchill flunked sixth grade and several college courses.

- Albert Einstein did not speak until he was four years old and couldn't read until he was seven. The Zurich Polytechnic refused to admit him because he 'showed no promise'.

- Robert Burns was an illiterate country boy. Cursed by poverty, he grew up to be a drunkard.

- Helen Keller became deaf, dumb and blind shortly after birth.

When you win, nothing hurts
Joe Nameth

GOAL SETTING

Extract of a conversation between 'Alice' and the 'Cheshire Cat' from 'Alice Through The Looking Glass'.

'Would you tell me, please, which way I ought to go from here?'
'That depends a good deal on where you want to get to,' said the Cat.
'I don't much care where,' said Alice, 'so long as I get somewhere.'
'Then it doesn't matter which way you go,' said the Cat.

Alice Through The Looking Glass - Lewis Carroll.

You become successful
the moment you start moving towards a worthwhile goal

GOAL SETTING

WHY YOU SHOULD SET GOALS

To achieve your definition of success you need to set goals. Goals are the stepping stones to your definition of success.

SUCCESSFUL PEOPLE SET GOALS

(really successful people write them down)

Until you commit your goals to paper, your intentions are seeds without soil

Zig Ziglar

GOAL SETTING
WHY PEOPLE DON'T SET GOALS

- If they do not achieve them, other people will think they have failed
- If they do achieve them, others may not like the way they have changed
- Setting goals means leaving their comfort zone
- Goals move them towards things they would rather not have to deal with
- They are afraid of what they might get or might lose
- They fail to plan, but always plan to act ... someday
- They think dreams are the same as goals

If you want to discover new oceans you must first have the courage to leave shore
Winston Churchill

GOAL SETTING
MAKE THEM MEASURABLE

Using the information you completed earlier you can now write goals to help you:

- Achieve your personal definition of success
- Satisfy your ideal roles
- Satisfy your motivators

Remember, your goals should be:

- Written in the present/positive tense, eg:
  - 'I am ...',
  - 'On dd/mm/yy I will ...',
  - 'By dd/mm/yy I will have ...'
    and **not**
  - 'I will ...' or 'I don't ...'
- S M A R T

> *There is no guarantee of reaching a goal at a certain time, but there is a*
> *guarantee of never attaining goals that are never set*
>
> **David McNally**

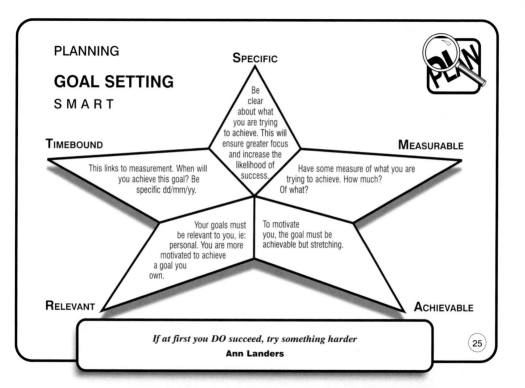

PLANNING

GOAL SETTING

S M A R T

SPECIFIC

Be clear about what you are trying to achieve. This will ensure greater focus and increase the likelihood of success.

TIMEBOUND

This links to measurement. When will you achieve this goal? Be specific dd/mm/yy.

MEASURABLE

Have some measure of what you are trying to achieve. How much? Of what?

Your goals must be relevant to you, ie: personal. You are more motivated to achieve a goal you own.

To motivate you, the goal must be achievable but stretching.

RELEVANT

ACHIEVABLE

If at first you DO succeed, try something harder
Ann Landers

PLANNING

GOAL SETTING
THREE AT A TIME

Review all your goals and select the three
most important ones; the goals that
will make the biggest difference to
you when you have achieved them.

(To retain focus and increase the
likelihood of success only work
on three goals at a time.)

In order to achieve these long-term
goals you need to break them down.

*The more balls you try and juggle, the more likely you're
going to drop them all*

GOAL SETTING
GOAL FUNNEL

Narrow down exactly what
it is you need to do to achieve
your personal definition of success
on a daily basis.

Definition of Success

Long-term Goals

Medium-term Goals

Short-term
Goals

Daily
Tasks

Obstacles are those things you see when you do not focus on your goals

GOAL SETTING

GOAL FUNNEL

	Medium-term goal	Short-term goal
Goal 1		
Goal 2		
Goal 3		

In order to achieve your short-term goals, break them down into daily activities.
Enter these activities into your time planner or diary.

*Many things which cannot be overcome when they are together, yield
themselves up when taken little by little*

Plutarch

GOAL SETTING

DAILY ACTIVITIES

You may find it hard to think of the daily activities. Imagine you have not achieved your goal and ask yourself what could have made the difference:

"IF ONLY I HAD ..."

Then write down what you wish you had done.

If you only have one or two activities that is OK. (As you will see, the closer you get to your goal the easier it becomes to see what you need to do to achieve it.)

Transfer these daily activities into your time planner or diary.

No problem can withstand the power of sustained creative thought

GOAL ACHIEVEMENT

Goal achievement is not a theoretical process that you can learn from a book.

It is a process requiring ACTION ...

The problem in my life and other people's lives is not the absence of knowing what to do, but the absence of doing it

Peter Drucker

SUCCESS CYCLE

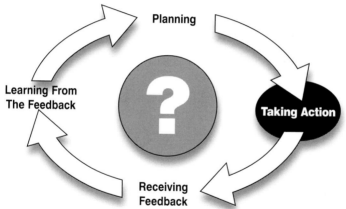

Planning

Taking Action

Receiving Feedback

Learning From The Feedback

?

I couldn't wait for success so I went ahead without it
Jonathan Waters

GOAL ACHIEVEMENT
ACCEPT YOUR MISTAKES

You cannot tackle your goals without errors, foul-ups and some fumbling along the way. No matter how clear your vision is, how detailed your plan, when you take action there will still be mistakes and oversights.

It is important to have the right strategy and be willing to live with some mistakes.

Your biggest mistake would be to wait until you believe you can take action free of any problems.

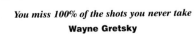

You miss 100% of the shots you never take
Wayne Gretsky

GOAL ACHIEVEMENT

THREE STEPS

1. Diagnose the present situation. Ensure you understand it. (Pages 7-11)
2. Build a vision for the future. What would be a successful outcome? (Pages 12-15)
3. Develop an action plan to move from 1 to 2. (Pages 22-29)

Now you are ready to take action.

Life does not require us to be the biggest or the best, it asks only that we try

TAKING ACTION

GOAL ACHIEVEMENT
IT'S UP TO YOU

This book cannot take action for you (although when you do act you will find some techniques to help you in the 'Success toolkit' in the final section).

Only **you** can take action so, in the words of a famous advertisement for a training shoe company:

JUST DO IT!

When you take action it will involve change. This book can help you cope with that change.

You may be disappointed if you fail, but you are doomed if you don't try
Beverley Sills

MANAGING CHANGE

THE CHANGE CYCLE

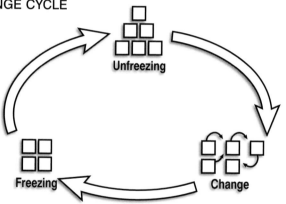

You see things; and you say, 'Why?' But I dream things that never were; and I say, 'Why not?'

George Bernard Shaw

MANAGING CHANGE
REDUCING RESISTANCE TO CHANGE

- Be flexible — Recognise that people do change. Develop new skills. Be prepared to let go of old skills and habits.

- Be confident — Focus on your strengths. Remember the changes you have handled successfully in the past.

- Recognise negative feelings — Think about the underlying reasons for doubts and fears - how realistic are those fears?

- Be aware — Recognise the amount of change in your life. Stagger **major** changes. (Remember, everything in this world exists as a consequence of some change.)

- Find support — Talk to colleagues, friends and relatives. Tell them about the changes and discuss your feelings.

Resisting change takes effort - find more productive ways to spend your energy!

Problems are the price of progress - don't bring me anything but problems
Charles Kettering

MANAGING CHANGE

TACTICS FOR IMPLEMENTING CHANGE

- Manage your thinking - If you expect problems, then you are likely to encounter them. Learn ways of gaining a 'breathing space' to reflect on what is happening.

- Enlist help - Find and use a mentor. Ask for help and advice along the way.

- Demonstrate success - Implement moderate risk changes first, to ensure that there is a greater chance of success.

- Chunk it - Go for incremental changes, rather than 'big bangs'. (Evolution lasts longer than revolution.)

To escape criticism - do nothing, say nothing, be nothing
Elbert Hubbard

MANAGING CHANGE

FORCE FIELD ANALYSIS

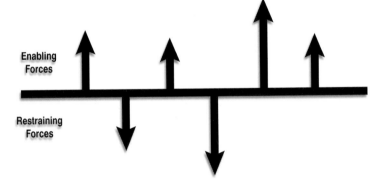

Enabling Forces

Restraining Forces

The pessimist sees difficulty in every opportunity. The optimist sees opportunity in every difficulty
Winston Churchill

MANAGING CHANGE

FORCE FIELD ANALYSIS

The term 'force field' comes from research by social scientist Kurt Lewin. He observed that any present state is in a condition of equilibrium between the forces pushing for, and the forces resisting, change.

'Force Field Analysis' sets out these forces in a diagram showing their direction and strength.

Complete an analysis for each area of change you wish to implement.

Concentrate on understanding and influencing the 'restraining forces'. Only then can you work with your 'enabling forces' to implement the change.

We cannot direct the wind but we can adjust the sails

MANAGING CHANGE
KÜBLER-ROSS CHANGE CURVE

INTEGRATION/
ACCEPTANCE

DENIAL

ANGER/
FRUSTRATION

SHOCK

DECISIONS/
PLANNING

EXPERIMENT/TESTING
NEW BEHAVIOURS

LOSS OF SELF-CONFIDENCE/DEPRESSION

*Life is about moving,
it's about change. And when things stop doing that they're dead*

40

TAKING ACTION

MANAGING CHANGE
KÜBLER-ROSS CHANGE CURVE

- The curve focuses on the effect of change on you

- Change is continuous, the end of one curve is the start of another

- When you experience change you will go through a series of phases

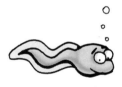

> *The ultimate measure of a man is not where he stands in moments of comfort and convenience, but where he stands at times of challenge and controversy*
>
> **Martin Luther King Jr**

MANAGING CHANGE
KÜBLER-ROSS CHANGE CURVE

Phase 1 - Shock
- Things seem unpredictable and uncontrollable
- You start to question: "This isn't what I expected?" "Why did I start this?"

Phase 2 - Denial
- You retreat into the past, giving a temporary feeling of being back in control
- In extreme cases you may not move beyond this point

Phase 3 - Anger/Frustration
- Gradual realisation of change makes you feel confused about what to do/how to cope
- You may feel disorganised and chaotic and remark: "I'm not sure what to do"

Phase 4 - Loss of Self-confidence/Depression
- The realisation of change hits home
- Your sense of control reduces, resulting in a feeling of powerlessness
- You will have difficulty in initiating activity

We don't see things as they are, we see them as we are
Anais Nin

MANAGING CHANGE

KÜBLER-ROSS CHANGE CURVE

Phase 4 - Loss of Self-confidence/Depression (cont'd)
- If this phase deepens or is prolonged, your feeling of self-worth could be seriously impaired

Phase 5 - Experiment/Testing new behaviours
- You accept the situation and are determined to see it through
- You start to let go of the past and have feelings of renewal, growth, excitement
- You initiate lots of activity, often without thought, which can lead to frustration

Phase 6 - Decisions/Planning
- You try to make sense of what has happened, balancing past experiences with new thoughts
- This is a period of reflection and sharing insights

Phase 7 - Integration/Acceptance
- Things now appear more stable
- You have a sense of direction and control

In the middle of every difficulty lies opportunity

MANAGING CHANGE
KÜBLER-ROSS CHANGE CURVE

Not everyone will flow through the curve smoothly.

 Some will fast forward.

 Some will backtrack.

 Some will get stuck in the early stages, because they refuse to change.

 Some will ignore their past experiences and start experimenting first.

 Some will get confused and locked in, as they deal with stressful situations in a diffuse way.

As you take action you will receive feedback which will help you follow your course through the curve. As you move along the curve, be aware of where you are, how you are feeling and how to move forward.

We cannot become what we need to be by remaining what we are
Max DePee

SUCCESS CYCLE

Planning

Taking Action

Learning From
The Feedback

Receiving
Feedback

?

I am convinced that life is 1% what happens to me and 99% how I react to it
Charles Swindoll

45

INTRODUCTION

Feedback will tell you whether you have been successful or not.

Successful feedback is easier to accept. However, it is unlikely you will succeed on your first attempt (when you do refer to page 51). Until then:

- Good planning and a positive attitude will not always prevent things from going wrong.

- When they do go wrong, do you laugh or cry? Either would be an understandable emotion after all your work and effort.
  - Crying is cleansing - laughter is healing.
  - Laughter will also prevent you from blowing the problem out of all proportion.

- Anger and resentment offer no benefit, so you may as well laugh, get over it and learn from it.

No cases of eyestrain have been developed by looking on the bright side of things

FAILURE

Unsuccessful feedback is not failure. **Failure is a reaction, not an outcome**. It is your reaction to feedback that will determine your success or failure.

Changing the goal, redefining success or not taking any corrective action is failure.

How different would your life be if you accepted all feedback as failure? I will give £1,000 to anyone who, on their first attempt, could:

- Walk
- Drive a car
- Play a tune on an instrument
- Ride a bicycle

- Pass every exam/test
- Talk fluently
- Write their name
- Tie their shoelaces

We learn from feedback, but our culture does not like it, or forgive those that make mistakes.

> *If you have made mistakes ... there is always another chance for you ... you may have a fresh start any moment you choose, for this thing we call 'failure' is not the falling down, but the staying down*
>
> **Mary Pickford**

NOTES

Don't think it, ink it

SUCCESS CYCLE

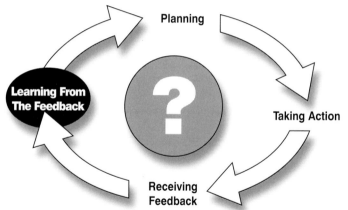

Planning

Taking Action

Receiving
Feedback

Learning From
The Feedback

?

You may have to fight a battle more than once to win it
Margaret Thatcher

49

WHEN THINGS GO WRONG

Focus on the causes, not the symptoms. Was it due to:

- Poor planning?
- A lack of commitment?
- A lack of support?
- A lack of time?
- Self-doubt?

It is important to learn from the problems and grow stronger. Adjust your plan, overcome the problem and forge ahead.

Everything looks like a failure in the middle

WHEN THINGS GO RIGHT

Focus on the causes, not the symptoms. Was it due to:

- Good planning?
- Commitment?
- Support of a mentor?
- Time invested?
- Self-belief?

It is important to learn from the successes and grow stronger too. Adjust your plan, maintain and build on your success and forge ahead. Celebrate your successes, so you are more likely to repeat them.

It is wise to keep in mind that no success or failure is necessarily final

NOTES

All achievements, all riches, have their beginnings in an idea

SUCCESS CYCLE

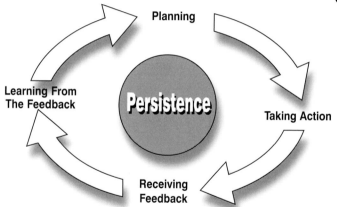

Planning

Taking Action

Receiving Feedback

Learning From The Feedback

Persistence

If you are persistent you normally arrive. It's the old tortoise and hare story
Noel Lister

53

INTRODUCTION

The success cycle revolves around your persistence:

- Persistence in planning your actions
- Persistence in carrying through those actions
- Persistence to learn from the feedback your actions bring and, most importantly ...
- The persistence to keep going when family and friends highlight your 'failures' (unsuccessful feedback)

Most people give up just when they're about to achieve success.
They quit on the one-yard line. They give up at the last minute of the game
one foot from a winning touch

H. Ross Perot

FAMOUS FAILURES?

(BUT FOR PERSISTENCE ...)

- Chester Carlson took four years and rejections from IBM, GE and RCA before the Haloid Company took his invention and renamed their company Xerox after it.
- James Dyson took five years and 5,127 prototypes to invent the world's first bag-less vacuum cleaner. Before he manufactured it he nearly became bankrupt, due to the worldwide patent fees. He is now on his way to becoming Britain's first billionaire inventor.
- Thomas Edison had 7,000 failed attempts to design a latex rubber plant and 11,000 failed experiments before he invented the electric light bulb. When he died he had 1,052 patents in his name.
- Walt Disney went to 312 banks before he secured backing for his cartoon animations. He was also bankrupt seven times.
- John Creasey received 753 publishers' rejections before the first of his 550 books was published.
- Marconi's friends had him institutionalised when he announced he could send messages through the air without the aid of wires or other physical means of communication.

> *Many people dream of success. To me success can only be achieved through repeated failure and introspection. In fact, success represents 1% of your work which results from 99% that is called failure*
> **Soichiro Honda**

FAMOUS FAILURES?
(BUT FOR PERSISTENCE ...)

- Failed in business 1831
- Ran for legislature and lost 1832
- Failed in business again 1834
- Sweetheart died 1835
- Had nervous breakdown 1836
- Lost second political race 1838
- Defeated for Congress 1843
- Defeated for Congress again 1846
- Defeated for Congress yet again 1848
- Defeated for U.S. Senate 1855
- Defeated for Vice President 1856
- Defeated for U.S. Senate 1858

Abraham Lincoln, elected sixteenth President of America 1860

I am not judged by the number of times I fail, but by the number of times I succeed. And the number of times I succeed is in direct proportion to the number of times I can fail and keep trying

Tom Hopkins

THE ESSENTIAL INGREDIENT

Nothing in the world can take the place of persistence.
Talent will not; nothing is more common than
Unsuccessful men with talent. Genius will not;
Unrewarded genius is almost a proverb.
Education will not; the world is full of educated derelicts.
Persistence and determination alone are omnipotent.

Calvin Coolidge

Never, never, never, never, never, never, never give up
Winston Churchill

NOTES

A man is as big as the measure of his thinking

SUCCESS TOOLKIT

The people who get on in this world are the people who get up and look for the circumstances they want and, if they can't find them, make them

George Bernard Shaw

INTRODUCTION

There are many techniques in your toolkit that can help you move towards your goals and your personal definition of success:

Time management
page 61 onwards

Focus
page 63 onwards

Belief systems
page 65 onwards

Affirmations
page 72 onwards

Visualisation
page 76 onwards

Luck
page 79 onwards

Modelling
page 81 onwards

Motivators
page 83 onwards

Input/Output
page 86 onwards

The environment you fashion out of your thoughts, your beliefs, your ideals, your philosophy, is the only climate you will ever live in

Albert A Montapert

TIME MANAGEMENT

To help you plan, remember the 'Pareto Principle':

80% of your success will come from 20% of what you do.

80% of Time Available → **20%** of the Results

20% of Time Available → **80%** of the Results

To help you plan your time effectively use this model:

IMPORTANCE

URGENCY		Low	High
	High	Ask someone else to do it ❷	Do it now ❶
	Low	Don't do it ❹	Do it later ❸

PRIORITY ❶❷❸❹

If you fail to plan, you're planning to fail

TIME MANAGEMENT

"How do I fit in the daily activities to achieve my goals?"

You must first realise:

- You cannot save time - you have all the time there is
- You will not have more time tomorrow, or in the future

Only then can you start to plan what to do with the time you have.

Spend 10 minutes at the end of each day, or at the beginning of each day, planning out your day. (Include your daily activities to achieve your goals.)

This planning session will kick-start your day and give you a greater sense of achievement at the end of the day.

At the end of the day review your success by asking: *"What have I done today to move towards my goals?"*.

Procrastination is opportunity's natural assassin
Victor Kiam

FOCUS

A goal set and never looked at will never be achieved.

As all good runners know, you move in the direction you are looking. This is why they focus on the finish line (rather than on their competitors).

Look at your goals daily, to keep focused. This will help you move towards them. For example, last time you bought a new style/model of car, did you notice how they suddenly appeared to be everywhere?

The reality is they were always there, you just never spotted them.

There are many opportunities out there for you to take advantage of. Until you become focused on your goals, you will not notice them. So, **review your goals daily** to keep focused.

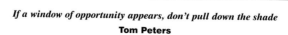

If a window of opportunity appears, don't pull down the shade
Tom Peters

FOCUS

A light can illuminate a room.

When it becomes focused it becomes a laser.
As a laser it can cut through steel.

Develop your **'laser thinking'** - devote time to review your goals and create a list of daily actions.

Where is your focus?

No wind blows fair for a ship without a destination
Old nautical proverb

SUCCESS TOOLKIT

BELIEF SYSTEMS

*If you **think** you are beaten, you are.*
*If you **think** you dare not, you don't.*
*If you like to win, but you **think** you can't,*
It is almost certain you won't.

*If you **think** you'll lose, you're lost,*
For out of the world we find,
Success begins with a fellow's will -
*It's all in the **state of mind**.*

*If you **think** you are outclassed, you are,*
*You've got to **think** high to rise,*
*You've got to **be sure of yourself** before*
You can ever win a prize.

Life's battles don't always go
To the stronger or faster man,
But soon or late the man who wins
Is the man WHO THINKS HE CAN!

Source unknown

Cogito, ergo sum
(I think, therefore I am)
Descartes

65

BELIEF SYSTEMS

If you have ever been to a circus you may have seen an elephant in a leg iron tethered by a small rope to a stake in the ground.

Have you ever stopped to wonder how this powerful beast is restrained by such a small stake?

When they are young, elephants are tethered to immovable stakes. For several weeks they struggle to free themselves. They soon learn they cannot escape.

Once they stop struggling a small stake is used to restrain them, because they believe they cannot escape.

All that power, energy and potential restrained by a belief that they cannot escape - the stake only serves to reinforce the belief.

As a person thinketh .. so are they

James Allen

BELIEF SYSTEMS
LIMITING BELIEFS

How often do you think:

I'm so stupid

I'm useless at ....

Why does it always happen to me?

It's easy for you

I'm so unlucky

I'll never be able to do that

People can't be trusted

I was never any good at ...

All your power, energy and potential restrained by a belief you cannot escape. Guess what happens when you think like this ...?

If you keep on saying things are going to be bad you have a good chance of becoming a prophet

BELIEF SYSTEMS

LIMITING BELIEFS

Example: playing golf

Limiting belief
"I never win"

"I was right"

I don't practise much
"What's the point"

"I lose"

I imagine losing
"They'll play better than me"

"I play worse"

I focus on my bad shots
"I always do that"
(more self-limiting
beliefs creep in)

"I play half heartedly"

"I lose motivation"

Alternatively

68

There is nothing either good or bad, but thinking makes it so
William Shakespeare

BELIEF SYSTEMS
ENABLING BELIEFS

How often will you think:

I'm clever	*I'm so lucky*
I'm good at ...	*I can do that*
I achieve my goals	*People are so reliable*
It is easy, isn't it?	*I'm getting better at ... every day*

All your power, energy and potential free to
stampede towards your goals.

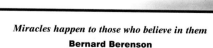

Miracles happen to those who believe in them
Bernard Berenson

69

BELIEF SYSTEMS
ENABLING BELIEFS

Enabling belief
"I have the potential to win"

I practise as much as possible
(to turn my potential into ability)

I imagine winning
"I'm as good as they are"

"I gain motivation
and confidence"

"I play to win"

I focus on my good shots
"Another Birdie"
(more enabling beliefs surface)

"I play better"

"I win"

"I was right"

---

*To succeed you have to believe in something with such passion
that it becomes a reality*

Anita Roddick

BELIEF SYSTEMS

A traveller was walking from one village to the next, when he came across an old man by the side of the road. He asked the old man "What is it like in the next village?". The old man promised to tell him once the traveller had told him what it was like in the village he had just left. The traveller explained "Terrible. I am glad to have left, the people were cold and unwelcoming". The old man explained the next village was much the same. The traveller, feeling disappointed, went on his way.

A few weeks later another traveller, walking the same way, came across the old man. "What is it like in the next village?", he asked. The old man promised to tell him once the traveller had told him what it was like in the village he had just left. The traveller explained "Wonderful, I am sorry to have left, the people were so warm and friendly". The old man explained the next village was much the same. The traveller, feeling excited, hurried on his way.

Life is what your thoughts make it
Marcus Aurelius

AFFIRMATIONS

INTRODUCTION

Affirmations are short, positive declarations or self-instructions. Repeated often they will change limiting beliefs into enabling beliefs and change you into the person you want to be.

To make affirmations work for you, you will need to write them down and repeat them to yourself out loud, with feeling, several times a day for 21 days. (Research has proven it takes 21 days for us to be comfortable with something new.)

Over the 21 days you will find yourself adjusting your behaviour in line with your affirmations. By the end of the three weeks the behaviour will be natural and you can start with new affirmations.

> *The greatest discovery of my generation is that you can change your circumstances by changing your attitude of mind*
>
> **William James**

SUCCESS TOOLKIT

AFFIRMATIONS

EXAMPLES

- I review my affirmations at least three times a day, and with each day I am becoming the person I want to be
- I review my goals daily and take positive action to achieve them
- I am lucky, good things are always happening to me
- I do the most productive thing possible at any given moment
- I am responsible
- I eat and drink healthily
- Something good will happen to me today
- I prepare thoroughly for everything I do

Your life is formed from the inside out

AFFIRMATIONS

RULES

1. Don't worry about how truthful your affirmations are. They are about who you are becoming, not who you are now.

2. State your affirmations in the present tense, eg: *I am ...* or *I always ...* rather than *I will ...*. (If you are uncomfortable with this, remember Rule 1 and/or alternatively use *Each day I am becoming ...*).

3. Pack them with positive emotion, eg: *I am fit and healthy because I exercise three times a week* rather than *I must exercise three times a week*. Avoid negatives, eg: *I don't ...* as this focuses on the behaviour you are trying to change. Your subconscious cannot recognise negatives and you, therefore, tell yourself to act on the behaviour you are trying to change.

4. Use no more than 10 affirmations at any one time.

5. Replace affirmations that are part of your behaviour with new ones that you want to achieve. From time to time review original affirmations to ensure they remain part of your behaviour.

The very act of believing creates strength of its own

AFFIRMATIONS
RULES

6. If you catch yourself contradicting your affirmations, say 'stop' and mentally remove yourself from the situation, relax and restate your affirmation.

7. You cannot stop the little voice inside your head telling you to succeed or fail, so you might as well teach it to tell you to succeed.

8. Affirmations will not work if you decide they will not work, as that is what your little voice will tell you. (Therefore, make one of your first affirmations a statement about how you use them and how they work.)

Start making affirmations work for you by writing them onto index cards, carrying them with you at all times and repeating them out loud to yourself, with feeling, several times a day for 21 days.

Your behavior is a reflection of what you truly believe
Hyrum Smith

VISUALISATION

With Olympic trials rapidly approaching, world class pentathlete Marilyn King lay in a hospital bed. Her injuries prevented her from training.

In place of 'real' training she substituted visualisation.

She re-ran her best performances in her head, pictured herself training and being selected for the Olympics.

When she was able to resume 'real' training her coach declared her to be almost completely fit.

Where there is no vision the people perish

Proverbs 29:18

VISUALISATION

Visualisation can be used to rehearse mentally for **any** situation.

The subconscious mind cannot differentiate between what is real and what it believes is real, ie: a vividly imagined experience - visualisation.

'Tricking' the subconscious in this way will make you feel more comfortable when the situation arises. You will know what to say and do.

By mentally rehearsing or visualising every possibility, you can eliminate fear and greatly increase your chance of success.

The only limits are, as always, those of vision
James Broughton

SUCCESS TOOLKIT

VISUALISATION

USE YOUR SENSES

When you use visualisation to prepare for a future event, like achieving your goals, you should use the three key senses:

What you see   - Who is there?
         What is happening?
         Look around - take in the details.

What you hear   - What are you saying?
         What are others saying?
         What other sounds are there in the background?

What you feel   - Who/what can you reach out and touch?
         How do you feel?
         How do others feel?

Use the other senses - smell and taste as appropriate.

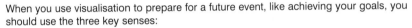

All men dream: but not equally. Those who dream by night in the dusty recesses of their minds wake in the day to find that it was vanity: but the dreamers of the day are dangerous men, for they may act their dreams with open eyes, to make it possible **T. E. Lawrence**

LUCK

Your subconscious mind acts on thought impulses. It can create physical realities from those impulses (as you have seen, in the section on beliefs). When they say 'You make your own luck', it's true.

There are millions of people who believe they are doomed because of 'bad luck' they believe they have no control over.

Dr. Christopher Peterson, Ph.D, an associate professor of psychology at the University of Michigan found that, over the course of a year, a confirmed pessimist was twice as likely to experience illness as an optimist.

Good luck can be created ...

You carry your own weather around with you
Stephen Covey

LUCK

If you were not prepared you would not spot the opportunity and/or you would be unable to take advantage of the opportunity.

You make your own luck!

People call me lucky. It's a funny thing, but the harder I work, the luckier I get

J. Paul Getty

MODELLING
INTRODUCTION

'If they can do it, so can I!'.

Modelling is the method by which you can do it.

As a baby you were an expert at modelling.

As you grew up you lost the skill.

Here's a reminder on how to do it.

You have to do it by yourself, but you can't do it alone
Martin Rutte

SUCCESS TOOLKIT

MODELLING
HOW TO

1. Identify the specific skill/behaviour that you want to reproduce

2. Find a person who is successful at this specific skill/behaviour

3. Observe them and notice what they do and how they do it

4. Question them about their skill/behaviour in detail, until you understand what they do - the process, how they do it and why they do each part of the process in that sequence

5. Reproduce the skill/behaviour by modelling the process

6. Check the process works

A candle loses nothing by lighting another candle
Father James Keller

MOTIVATORS

As well as using your motivators to **define** the success you want to attain, you can use your key motivators to help you **achieve** success.

When you use affirmations, visualisation, focus, enabling beliefs, etc, use what will motivate you.

For example, if your goal was for your bodyweight to be a specified amount by a specified time, this may not seem to tie in with any of the motivators.

One can never consent to creep when one feels an impulse to soar
Helen Keller

MOTIVATORS

As well as focusing on the end result, the size you will be, think about what may motivate you and give you the energy and commitment you need:

1 Status   - The admiration and respect of family, friends and colleagues
                   Recognition for losing the most weight each week at a slimming club

2 Power   - Having others seek your advice and copy your technique
                   Attracting the opposite sex

3 Material   - Buying a new wardrobe, as all your old clothes no longer fit
   reward   Acquiring top of the range sports equipment to exercise with

4 Autonomy   - Making your own decisions about what you eat and how you exercise
                   Achieving your ideal weight **your** way

I refuse to recognise impossibilities. I cannot discover that anyone knows enough about anything on this earth to say what is and what is not possible

Henry Ford

MOTIVATORS

5   Expertise -   Acquiring specialist knowledge of food, a sport, the body
                      Obtaining a qualification and/or having others seek your expertise

6   Creativity -   The unique way you will achieve your goal
                      Sharing **your** method to benefit others

7   Affiliation -   The new friends and relationships you will establish through a
                      slimming club or a sports club

8   Search for -   Why you want to be a particular weight and the meaning behind this
     meaning   How you will feel and how others will feel about you

9   Security   -   Making incremental changes which can be maintained
                      Working with a group of like-minded people
                      Maintaining your new weight

If you do anything just for the money you don't succeed
Barry Hearn

85

INPUT/OUTPUT

INTRODUCTION

There is an old computer saying:

 RUBBISH IN  RUBBISH OUT

So, be aware of what you put (input) into your brain (computer).

Also, be aware of your 'output'. What you give out will come back to you tenfold (remember the travellers on page 71).

> *I was going to buy a copy of 'The Power of Positive Thinking', and then I thought: What the hell good would that do!*
>
> **Ronnie Shakes**

SUCCESS TOOLKIT

INPUT/OUTPUT

INPUT

- Listen to motivational tapes
- Read motivational books

- Find and use a role model
- Find and use a mentor
- Listen to good 'upbeat' music
- Watch/listen to comedy/comedians
- Be aware of/filter media messages

- Seek advice and feedback from others
- Mix with people who do/have what you want to do/have
- Mix with successful people
- Read your goals/affirmations
- Use visualisation
- Focus on success
- Record your successes to review during negative periods

Start every day with an inspiring thought

INPUT/OUTPUT

OUTPUT

- Smile
- Learn to laugh
- Treat others how they want to be treated
  (not how you want others to treat you)
- Praise others
- Share your successes
- If you love someone, tell them
- Show you care
- Give people small personal gifts
- Help others to achieve success
- Become a mentor or role model
- Be polite and courteous
- Share your goals

Give, and it will be given to you
Luke 6:38

ROLE MODEL

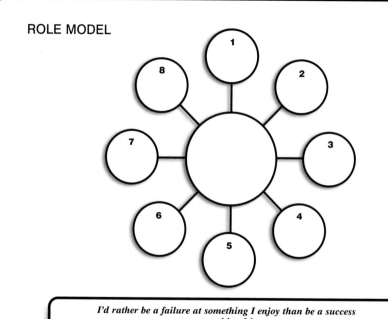

I'd rather be a failure at something I enjoy than be a success at something I hate

George Burns

A FINAL THOUGHT ...

It is not the critic who counts; not the man who points out how the strong man stumbles, or where the doer of deeds could have done better. The credit belongs to the man who is actually in the arena, whose face is marred by dust, sweat and blood; who strives valiantly; who errs, and comes short again and again; who knows the great enthusiasms, the great devotions, who spends himself in a worthy cause; who at the best knows in the end the triumph of high achievement, and who at the worst, if he fails, at least fails while daring greatly, so that his place shall never be with those cold and timid souls who know neither victory nor defeat.

President Theodore Roosevelt
'The Man in the Arena' speech, Paris 1910

I've got a great ambition to die of exhaustion rather than boredom
Angus Grossart

About the Author

Paul Hayden, FinstSMM, MIFP, Dip PFS.
Paul runs his own training and consultancy business. His clients include KPMG, Bank of Scotland, IBM, Prudential and BusinessLink. In his role as a training consultant, Paul works to develop a wide range of skills and knowledge to help both people and companies maximise their potential.

Prior to running his own company, Paul worked at Allied Dunbar where he had responsibility for the development of head office personnel and, later, the salesforce. Paul is author of several in-house training manuals, 'The Learner's Pocketbook' and co-author of 'The Financial Adviser's Guide'.

Contact
Paul can be contacted through:
The Hayden Partnership, P O Box 965, Swindon, Wiltshire SN5 5YS.
Tel: 01793 772844 Fax: 01793 772844 Mobile: 07768 012316
E-mail: paul@haydenpartnership.com www.haydenpartnership.com

We cannot move at all, unless we are willing to accept losing our balance at least temporarily

ORDER FORM

Your details

Name _____

Position _____

Company _____

Address _____

_____

_____

Telephone _____

Fax _____

E-mail _____

VAT No. (EC companies) _____

Your Order Ref _____

Please send me:

		No. copies
The Personal Success	Pocketbook	☐
The _____	Pocketbook	☐
The _____	Pocketbook	☐
The _____	Pocketbook	☐
The _____	Pocketbook	☐

Order by Post
MANAGEMENT POCKETBOOKS LTD
LAUREL HOUSE, STATION APPROACH,
ALRESFORD, HAMPSHIRE SO24 9JH UK
Order by Phone, Fax or Internet
Telephone: +44 (0)1962 735573
Facsimile: +44 (0)1962 733637
E-mail: sales@pocketbook.co.uk
Web: www.pocketbook.co.uk

MANAGEMENT POCKETBOOKS